Swords
and
Bikes

T0321641

Contents

Written by Joseph Coelho

Illustrated by Jobe Anderson

Collins

1. Singing in the Night

The low gentle singing started not long
after Michaela's twelfth birthday.
Same time every night,
it was as if the night was chanting.

She peered down from her flat
on the third floor of Binley Towers
to the field opposite.
The field was part of the grounds
of Greenshire House,
a huge, old, abandoned mansion,
Now owned by the local university.
The signs staked into the ground
read "Keep out" and "Private property"
but that wouldn't stop Michaela and her friends.

The field led to a huge bush.
The roof of the huge old house
peeped up behind the huge bush.
The mansion was built
hundreds of years ago.

The huge bush kept the mansion
tangled up and locked away.
Michaela and her friends
would try to get near
but the groundskeeper
would yell
"Stay back! Stay back!"
The grounds keep would yell
"Stay back!"

Michaela was sure
that the singing she heard at night
was coming from that house.

2. Breakfast

Breakfast
– a steaming plate
of plantain and eggs.
Michaela asked her dad about the singing.

"Not this again Kayla, it's probably
just Gavin listening
to reggae next door
or could be upstairs
you know the Sloans snore
or it could be Gabby
doing aerobics below.
We've got neighbours all around,
anyone could be your singing show."

Michaela's father had
already warned Michaela to …
"stay away from Greenshire House"
after the groundskeeper
marched her and her friend Norris
up to their flats
and spoke to both their parents
about calling the police!

"You have plans today?" asked her Dad
serving up fried tomatoes.
"Probably play computer with Norris."
"You guys should go out,
you don't realise it when you're young
but summer ain't forever –
get out there and have some fun."

Michaela smiled guiltily –
she had begged her dad for her bike
but had only used it a handful of times.
She was too scared of falling off
and told her father as much.
Her father rubbed her 'fro,
planted a bristly kiss on her cheek.
"You have to be brave –
get on your bike and go!
It's only by facing our fears
that we find courage and grow!
I'm on a long shift today,
but I'll see you tonight.
There's curry in the fridge
that'll microwave-up just right."
But his words had stayed with her.
She would go out on her bike.

3. The Bush

Michaela and Norris met on their bikes
at the bottom of their block.
"Should we go up to the house?" asked Norris
squinting up at Michaela
under a shock of strawberry-blond hair.
"Did you hear the singing last night?"
asked Michaela, and Norris nodded.
Michaela and Norris cycled
towards the bush
that hid Greenshire House.
A field of green
rolled out ahead of them
free of the groundskeeper
but he could be watching.
"Let's be quick," said Michaela.

The bush was high, higher than a bus,
and tangled – more tangled than a bowl
of day-old spaghetti.
Michaela and Norris poked and prodded
trying to find a way through the tangles.
A noise from the campus made them stop.
"Phew … just students," said Michaela.
They got back to their searching
prodding and poking until …
"What's this?"

Norris was on his hands and knees
scraping the dirt at the base of the bush.

A wide rectangular stone was revealed.
"That looks like a step,"
said Michaela in astonishment.
"The bush is less tangled here," said Norris.
with stretched-out arms.
They felt the other steps rising up,
overgrown by the bush's tangle.

"I think I can push through," said Michaela
forcing an arm and then a shoulder
deeper into the devilish bush
her feet finding purchase
on one, then two steps.
But as she went deeper in,
a deep humming
vibrated through her,
into her bones, making her jump back.

"It's like the singing
I heard last night but deeper,"
said Michaela as the bush
drew them in deeper still.

There was a shout from behind.
The groundskeeper was running
all raised fist, red face,
his shouted words muffled
on the hot summer air.

"Quick, we need to go!" said Michaela.

They grabbed their bikes
and pushed them up
the overgrown stairs
and into the bush's depths.

4. The Other Side

The groundkeeper's shouts
were immediately replaced
by the deep humming of the bush
which got deeper and louder
the further into the bush they pushed.
Until! With a rush
they tumbled out the other side
and into a dilapidated Victorian garden.

They were faced with a red brick wall.
In a niche at its centre
was a marble fountain dry and disused.
At the top of the fountain
was a carved marble head
with a leering smiling face
and horns.

"Can you hear it?" asked Michaela,
"can you hear the singing?"

Norris's eyes went wide
as he took in the garden around him.
Michaela followed his gaze,
a brick summer house
old and crumbling stood to their left,
an empty pond to their right,
overgrown flower beds
with strange-looking plants
lined the red brick wall.

A host of stems and sucking vines
stretched up the red-brick wall.
But there was no source for the singing,
it was coming from all around,
from every flower, every blade of grass,
from every brick that made the red-brick wall
even from the marble of the fountain itself
and especially that glaring horned head.
"Let's wait for the groundskeeper
to leave, then we can get out."

They turned to the bush – the bush was gone
and in its place was a thick tumbling forest.

5. The Forest

"Where'd the bush go?" cried Norris as Michaela
rubbed her eyes in disbelief.
An endless forest stretched out
from where the bush once stood.
All crooked branches and mossy trunks
with trees crowding in on all sides,
vines creeping along their bark
like hungry leeches.

They turned back
to the red-brick wall and the fountain
with its grinning horned head.
"We have to get out," shouted Michaela
but the red-brick wall
stretched on forever
to their left and right.
"Climb over it," called Norris.
Michaela searched
for hand and foot holds
in the red-brick work
but as she climbed, the wall grew!
Getting taller and taller,
impossible to get over.

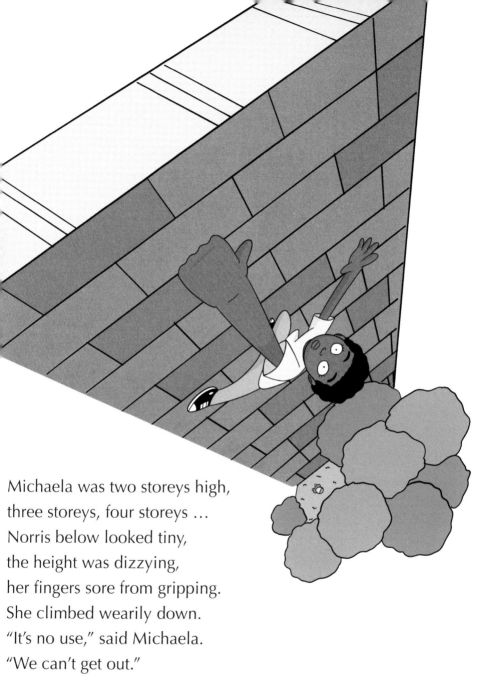

Michaela was two storeys high,
three storeys, four storeys …
Norris below looked tiny,
the height was dizzying,
her fingers sore from gripping.
She climbed wearily down.
"It's no use," said Michaela.
"We can't get out."

A rustling was heard in the trees,
far off in the distance at first,
then it got louder
                    and louder
                              and louder.
Suddenly a huge bristling creature
came crashing out of the forest.
It looked like a wolf, jet black in colour
but instead of a wolf's head
it had the head and beak of a crow!
And along the back of its wolf-like body
two large black wings flapped.

It gazed at Michaela and Norris
with gleaming green eyes,
before launching itself at the pair.
It grasped hold of the back of Norris's hoody
and, half-hopping, half-flying
dragged him back into
the forest's inky depths.

6. A Visitor in the Garden

Norris's bike was left
abandoned on the grass
in front of the fountain,
its wheels spinning.
Michaela called after him
as Norris's cries of, "HEEEEEELP!"
faded into the forest's gloom.
Michaela wanted to follow,
but she was too scared,
wanted to help her friend
but her legs were shaking
and that's when
she heard the singing.

In the ruined brick summer house
sat a creature in the shade.
At first Michaela could just make out
the glow of his green eyes,
but as she stared
she saw the shape of a man
come into focus.

A man sat crossed-legged on a bench.
His furry legs poked from his trousers,
ending in goat-like hooves.
On his human torso he was wearing
a funny-looking jacket of jade green
and in his hands he held a book.
But stranger than his hooves
stranger than his jade jacket
and the glamour of his green eyes
were the two large horns
that twisted out of his forehead.

7. Bugeja

Michaela wanted to run
but the only way out
was through the forest
and she was too scared
to go in there.

The green-eyed, horned man
stopped singing.

"If you're done being scared
I can help you and your friend," he said.

"Who are you?" stammered Michaela,
gripping the handlebars of her bike
extra tight.

"I am Bugeja, I do beg your pardon.
You have entered my realm
and this is my garden."

The man-goat pointed at the fountain –
the stone head with horns above it
was a sculpture of him.

Michaela took a few tentative steps forward,
wheeling her bike out ahead of her,
when suddenly the man leapt up
and trotted over to her.
In the sunlight
he didn't look quite as scary.

"You don't have to be scared," said Bugeja.
"I need your help."

"Help! What can I do –
I just lost my friend
to a wolf-crow thing
and I'm stuck in here!
And I don't know a thing."

"You don't have to worry –
it's all in here …
I have dreamed of you both.
And they were dreams of such cheer."

Bugeja opened his book.
It was full of handwritten
scrawlings, notes and pictures.
One picture in particular
looked like Michaela except for one thing –
she was dressed in a suit of wooden armour
and holding a glowing sword.

8. Armour

"I have been unable to leave my garden
because that beast that took your friend
has been eager to eat me!
Will this terror never end?
But then I dreamed of a saviour
that looks just like you
a hero for this forest
with a heart brave and true."

Bugeja flicked through his notebook
showing pictures of
Norris, Michaela and Bugeja
standing in front of Binley Towers.
"My dreams are mainly visions
but this I have seen again and again.
If you can go to save your friend
you can make this terror end.
No bravery will go unrewarded
I swear by the red of my bricks
if you do this little task
I will gift you with magic."

"Magic? What magic?
And if you're magic why can't you
defeat the crow-wolf?" asked Michaela.

"That beast is immune to my magic
every spell, and jinx and charm
but I can conjure you into a warrior
and you can deliver the harm!"

He twirled his fingers in the air
and vines popped out from the ground.
They twisted and tangled around Michaela –
her arms and legs,
her chest and back.

The vines thickened and covered her,
becoming … a wooden breastplate
and greaves for the legs,
bark gauntlets for the arms
and a helmet of thick mahogany.
"This is amazing," said Michaela
as she started to flex and bend
in her new wooden armour.
"I feel invincible."

"It will protect you from the beast,
but you must be careful –
there are many things in the forest
and all are hungry for a feast."

"What about the sword in your picture
– can I have that?"

"I don't have the sword
but you'll find it in the dark.
Follow the beast's fallen feathers
in your armour of magical bark.
Now go and save your friend
and make this terror end."

Michaela took a nervous gulp
as she gazed into the forest's depths.
The armour gave a new sense of courage.
She turned back to Bugeja
but he was gone.

9. Into the Forest

Moving in the armour
felt almost natural to Michaela,
and what's more with the armour on
she forgot all her fears
of falling from her bike.

There was a clear path
where the crow-wolf
had crashed through the undergrowth
and just like Bugeja had said
fallen feathers marked the way.

Michaela cycled slowly at first,
picking her way over the roots
of the forest but as she went on
the ground started to slope away downhill
and her bike started to speed up!
Over lumps and bumps and mounds in the ground,
Michaela skidded and swerved, twisted and turned.
Ducked under branches,
jumped old trunks and stumps.
Her bike going faster and faster
the fallen crow-wolf feathers
kicking up into the air as she went.

A squeaking chitter sounded above her –
a sound that put fear into her heart.

She glanced upwards and saw
squirrels –
but not normal squirrels,
they were carrying tiny bows and arrows
and they were firing …

Thunk! A tiny arrow struck Michaela's
wooden breastplate,
then another and another.
A scurry of squirrels
was leaping the branches
of the dark forest,
firing a volley of arrows.

Michaela could feel them
hitting the back of her wooden armour.
Luckily none of them
were strong enough
to pierce through to her skin.

Michaela pushed hard
onto her bike's pedals
and sped onwards
as the squirrels chased behind.

She got far out ahead of them
and started to form a plan.
She ducked under a huge branch
and skidded to a stop out of sight.

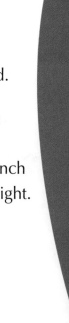

She bent the tree branch back as
far as it would go and waited.
The squirrels were getting closer,
closing the gap she had made.
Their chittering squeaks
ringing through the forest.
She saw them leaping her way,
bounding towards the bent branch,
and just when they were about to discover
her hiding place
she let the branch go!

THWACK!

It swished through the air
into the mass of scuttling squirrels,
sending them shooting off
into the depths of the dark forest.

10. A Cave

Michaela pulled the tiny
arrows from her armour
and looked around.
She was in front of a cave,
at its entrance was a pile
of crow-wolf feathers.

"This must be it – Norris must be inside,"
she whispered to herself
surprised at how brave she felt.
She took a deep breath
and entered the cave.

The cave smelt of damp and earth.
The opening was small so she left her bike
at the entrance and squeezed inside.
It was a tunnel twisting left and right.
Up and down,
zig-zagging this way and that.
Weird phosphorescent mushrooms
glowed pink on the walls
which helped light her way.

Had she been walking
for minutes or hours?
She couldn't tell.
In the dark gloom,
time seemed to have no meaning.
Eventually, the tunnel opened out
into a huge cavern.
On a stone platform at its centre was Norris.
He was tied up with his knees
bunched to his chest – shivering,
and with good reason.
The crow-wolf was circling around him
making its strange cawing-howl.

Michaela didn't know what to do.
She had to save her friend, but how?
That's when she saw it.
In a niche to her left
was a blue glow.
This glow was coming from a sword
that stood upright
with its blade stuck fast into the ground
making Michaela think of the story
of the *Sword in the Stone*.

"If I can get the sword, then perhaps
I can defeat the crow-wolf
and get Norris out of here,"
thought Michaela.
She started to creep towards the sword
using the shadows to hide
from the snarling, snapping beast.

11. The Glowing Sword

Michaela crept and creeped
creeped and crept
her way to the glowing sword,
trying to ignore the whimperings
of Norris who had no idea she was there,
or the caw-howling of the crow-wolf
who she hoped wouldn't spot her.

Michaela had never held a sword before.
What if it was too heavy for her?
What if it was stuck in the ground
like the sword in the story?
What if the crow-wolf spotted her
before she reached it?

All of these fears tumbled and rumbled
in Michaela's mind.
I have to be brave. She told herself
Just like Dad said …
it's the only way to grow.
I have to rescue Norris
and get us back home.

The sword was very close now.
The light of its blue glow was
falling upon her.
She'd have to be quick.
If she lingered in the light
the crow-wolf might spot her.

I'll make a run for it and grab the sword
and confront the crow-wolf with a heroic roar!
She took some deep breaths
and rushed to the sword.

She leapt through the air,
grabbed the sword and pulled.

12. The Wizard

A sound like thunder
rang through the cavern.
The sword lifted out of the ground,
Michaela rolled over the floor
and twisted herself towards the crow-wolf
with the glowing sword in hand.

"Let my friend go," she roared
at the feathered shaggy thing,
feeling the bravery in her chest
roll through her, warm and sweet.

"Michaela!" cried out Norris
as the crow-wolf turned
and fixed Michaela with a chilling
green-eyed stare and started to laugh.

The crow-wolf walked towards Michaela
but as it did so it started to transform.
Its back legs became more goat-like,
its front half became that of a man
and its head became horned.

Bugeja stood in front of Michaela,
his eyes glowing a wicked green.
"At last," he cackled.
"You have collected the sword for me."
"What do you mean? What are you?"
shouted Michaela, confused.

"I am a wizard trapped in this land,
I sang to lure you to my forest.
I used my magic to transform
and to drag Norris here
so that you would have the incentive
to find the sword,
for only a human could retrieve it
and only by retrieving the sword
can I open the gateway to your world
where I will use my magic
to take over everything."

Bugeja clicked his fingers
and stamped his hooves
and in a flash of bright green magic
they were all transported back to the garden.

13. The Garden

Michaela rubbed her eyes.
The green flash of magic
had blurred her vision temporarily.

They were back in the garden
Michaela's armour was gone
and the sword was now in Bugeja's hand.

"Why are you doing this?"
shouted Michaela – surprised that even though
her armour was gone, she still felt brave.

"I have been trying to break
into your world for centuries.
Nothing worked until I found
this place and its link
to the garden in your world.
But still I couldn't cross over
but my singing could
and I sang sweet songs
hoping to lure a human here
and trick them to retrieve
The Sword Of Dimensions –
an ancient and powerful artefact
capable of slicing its way
from my world into yours."

Michaela couldn't believe it.
By following the singing
she had unwittingly allowed a wizard
from a magical place
to break into the normal world.

She knew she should have stayed away
from Greenshire House,
should have listened to her dad.
Now Bugeja would use his magic
to take over everything
and it was all her fault.

Bugeja waved the sword
where the forest and garden met –
the trees started to shimmer
the trees started to change
and become … a bush …
the very same bush
that Norris and Michaela
had squeezed through
to get into the garden
of Greenshire House – and this magical world.
The dark forest was replaced
by the bush that Michaela and Norris
knew so well.

"That's it!" cackled Bugeja.
"Soon I will be able to enter your world
and humans shall bow to me."
He shot out his left hand
and danced his fingers in the air.
Strange root-like monsters
started to appear from the ground.

"He's making an army," whimpered Norris
as creature after creature rose up –
earth falling from their gnarled faces.

A rustling came from the bush –
someone or something was pushing through
from the normal world.
It was the groundskeeper
but he looked different:
his eyes danced with purple light
his clothes had changed to a scarlet robe
and he was holding a staff
of twisted silver metal.

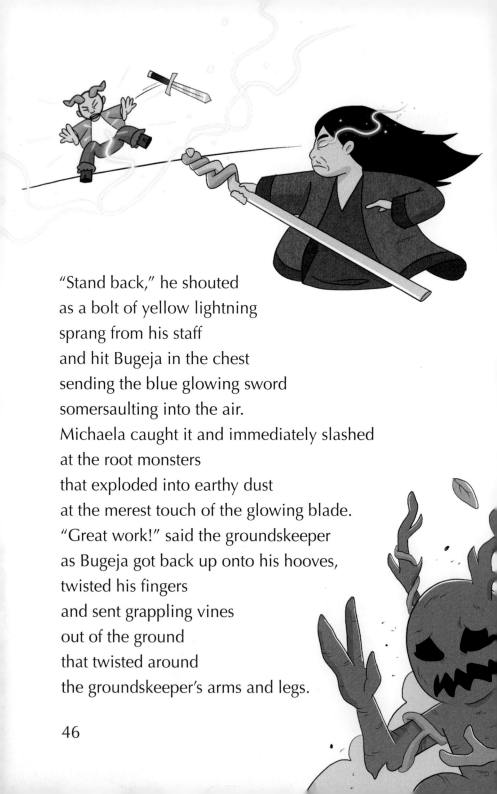

"Stand back," he shouted
as a bolt of yellow lightning
sprang from his staff
and hit Bugeja in the chest
sending the blue glowing sword
somersaulting into the air.
Michaela caught it and immediately slashed
at the root monsters
that exploded into earthy dust
at the merest touch of the glowing blade.
"Great work!" said the groundskeeper
as Bugeja got back up onto his hooves,
twisted his fingers
and sent grappling vines
out of the ground
that twisted around
the groundskeeper's arms and legs.

The groundskeeper muttered a spell
and in a flash of bright orange light,
Michaela was once again covered in armour,
but this time it was metal
and it wasn't just her!
Norris had armour too
and in his hands he had
a second glowing blue blade.
Together they slashed and hacked
through the root monsters
until all that was left
were many piles of steaming earth.
They turned to the two wizards –
the groundskeeper and Bugeja.
Bugeja was bound with metal cables
around his hands and hooves.

14. Back to Binley House

The groundskeeper approached.
"There is a very good reason why
I tell the local children
to stay away from Greenshire House.
There is an evil power
here and you two have found him.
I am Latimera, a wizard from this world,
but I work as a guardian in yours,
making sure that evil wizards like Bugeja
never manage to break through.
It's not just the ground and grass I protect,
I protect your world as you know it."

Latimera started to mutter more spells
turning the bush back into the dark forest
except for the stairway
that Michaela and Norris
had originally found.

"The stairs will take you back
down to your own world."

"We're sorry," mumbled Norris and Michaela
relieved to have been saved
but feeling bad for nearly
allowing Bugeja into their world.

"That's ok. You have both
proven yourselves handy
with a magical sword.
There may come a time
when I will need your help
to keep your world safe.
But until then, I shall keep hold
of your armour and weapons."
Latimera clicked his fingers
and the armour and swords disappeared.

What will happen to Bugeja?" asked Michaela,
feeling strangely bad for the wizard.

"Don't worry about him,
I will strengthen all the spells
to keep him trapped here.
But I expect you two
to tell all your friends –
stay well clear of Greenshire House
the fate of the world may depend on it."

Michaela and Norris
took the stairs through the overgrown bush
feeling a mix of relief and excitement.
As soon as they stepped out of the bush,
the magical portal zipped up behind them
and they were greeted
by the majesty of Binley Towers
looming above.

"Oh no – our bikes," said Norris,
suddenly realising
that their bikes had been abandoned
in the magical forest.
Suddenly a sparkling
filtered through the air.
Two brand-new bikes
appeared in front of them.

Bikes unlike anything they had ever seen
with levers and buttons,
gears of gold,
handlebars of brass.
A note tied to them read
"From Latimera – a little something to say thank you."

51

Michaela and Norris mounted
their new bikes.
The sun was still up in the sky.
It would be hours before
they were due home for tea.

"Should we give these a try?" asked Norris.
"Definitely," said Michaela.
"I want to go as fast as we possibly can."

They pushed down on their pedals
and sped the bikes
along the paths of their estate,
going faster and faster.
They whooped and cheered
and just when they thought
that their bikes couldn't get any better,
they each pressed a button on their handlebars
and to their delight
their bikes took flight.

Michaela's bravery

But his words had stayed with her.
She would go out on her bike.

Michaela wanted to follow,
but she was too scared,

and what's more with the armour on
she forgot all her fears
of falling from her bike.

and just when they were about to discover
her hiding place
she let the branch go!

She started to creep towards the sword
using the shadows to hide
from the snarling, snapping beast.

"Why are you doing this?"
shouted Michaela – surprised that even though
her armour was gone, she still felt brave.

Together they slashed and hacked
through the root monsters
until all that was left
were many piles of steaming earth.

"I want to go as fast as we possibly can."

55

Ideas for reading

Written by Jonny Walker
Specialist Teacher and Educational Consultant

Reading objectives
- explore how a poem can be used to tell a story
- make links between poems and children's own life experiences
- understand how poets use alliteration and onomatopoeia

Spoken language objectives
- ask relevant questions to extend their understanding and knowledge
- use relevant strategies to build their vocabulary
- articulate and justify answers, arguments and opinions
- give well-structured descriptions, explanations and narratives for different purposes, including for expressing feelings
- participate in performances

Curriculum links: Relationships Education: Families and people who care for me

Interest words: brave, private, satyr, trickery, alliteration, onomatopoeia

Talk before reading

- Look at the cover together and read the title and blurb. Focus on the word *brave* in the blurb and ask children to consider when they have been brave and faced their own fears.
- Point out that swords and bikes is an unusual pair of objects. What do children think might happen in the book?
- Explain that this book is a story in verse, which means it is a poem that tells a story. Consider together the strengths of using this form of writing for an adventure story (i.e. *shorter lines and more rhythm can add tension*).
- Ask children if they know any other books that have been written by Joseph Coelho.

Support personal responses

- Take time to discuss the poem after you have read it. Use the following questions or ask your own.
  - o Which part of the poem most surprised you?
  - o Why might somebody want to go to a place that is signposted as being *private*?